Green Beans,
Potatoes,
and Even
Tomatoes

to Mrs. Clarke, my third-grade teacher in Richfield, Minnesota
—B.P.C.

to my mom, who taught me that brussels sprouts were good
(when you had them for the zillionth time)
—M.G.

Vegetable:
A plant grown as food. Vegetables are usually eaten as side dishes or in salads.

Green Beans, Potatoes, and Even Tomatoes

What Is in the **Vegetables** Group?

by Brian P. Cleary

illustrations by Martin Goneau

consultant Jennifer K. Nelson, Master of Science,
Registered Dietitian, Licensed Dietitian

M Millbrook Press • Minneapolis

Sometimes we slice them

or dice them

or steam them.

Often we peel them,

bake them, or cream them.

Whether poured from a blender

or dipped at a party,

vegetables help us be healthy and hardy.

So what is a veggie?
It's a plant grown as food.

It's meant
to be nibbled
and tasted and chewed.

Though often a side dish,
this food group is key.

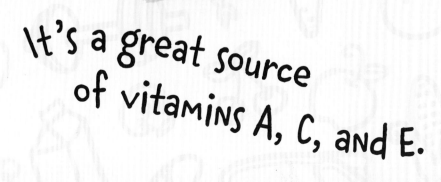

It's a great source
of vitamins A, C, and E.

Vitamin A
helps our eyes
and our skin.

Which vegetables have it?
You'll find that it's in

some spinach,
a warm sweet potato,
a carrot

so wholesome and tasty
you won't want to share it.

9

And what are the veggies with vitamin C?

Bell peppers,

brussels sprouts,

broccoli are three.

Cabbage that's red
and some white cauliflower

Get Your Vitamin C

HERE

$$$

help cuts and wounds heal
with their vitamin power!

Vitamin E keeps your
cells working hard.

CELLS AT WORK

You'll find it in veggies
including swiss chard.

Turnip and collard greens
some find delicious—

these vegetables listed
are very nutritious.

Vegetables won't be found
growing on trees

(that's only for fruits),

but you'll find them with ease

14

in rows on a farm
or a garden that's hoed;

at a stand—
fresh, not canned—
by the side of the road.

Whether they're raw

or they're cooked

or they're frozen,

hastily gathered
or carefully chosen,

16

vegetables have many colors and sizes.

Two cups every day's
what the doctor advises.

Folks for some time tried to get to the root

of whether tomatoes are "veggie" or "fruit."

Based upon how
they are eaten
and grown,

The Supreme Court declared
they are "veggie" alone.

The purplest vegetable you've ever seen

is what we call eggplant—
in French, aubergine.

Beans of all kinds offer fiber galore.

They help you digest

and to "toot" a bit more!

Some veggies are starchy,
like corn
or potatoes.

Some,
orange
or red,
like these squash or tomatoes.

22

Many,
like Spinach
and bok choy, are green.

Eat them,
and you'll be

a lean, green machine!

Look at potatoes,
and you'll see their eyes.

Corn grows in ears,
right on up to the skies.

cabbage and lettuce are both sold in heads.

Just like us,
vegetables lie in their beds.

While cucumbers often are
cut up in salads,

they come in
quite handy
for lip-synching ballads.

Celery comes in a stalk
and is used

in salads and soups
and in thick, tasty stews.

So take some to snack on

or gobble
or munch.

Add them to dinner
or breakfast or lunch.

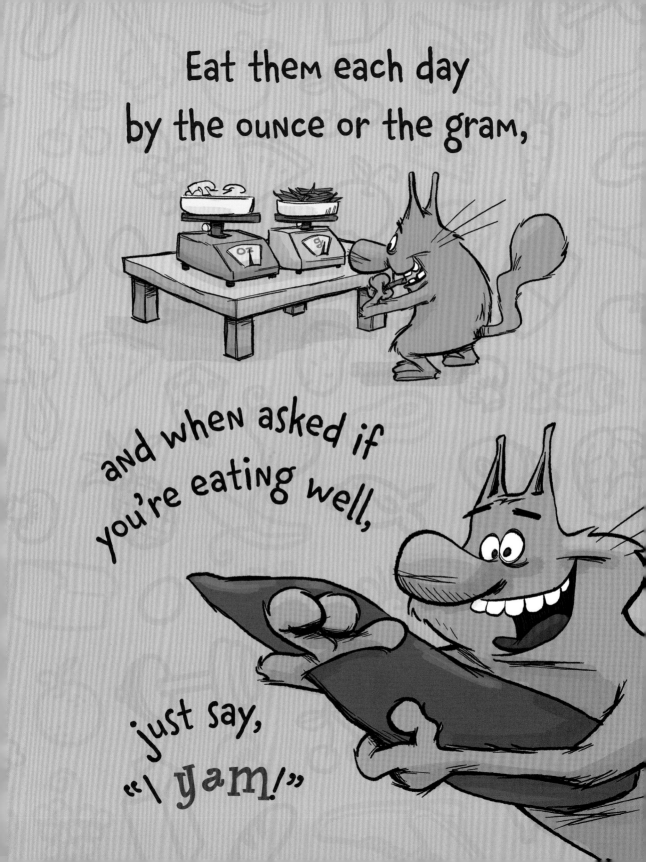

So what is in the vegetables group? Do you know?

You should eat 1.5 to 2.5 cups of vegetables every day. The exact amount depends on your age and how much exercise you get. To figure out the right amount for you, visit www.mypyramid.gov and click on MyPyramid Plan.

2 medium carrots equals 1 cup

1 medium potato equals 1 cup

1 large tomato equals 1 cup

1 large ear of corn equals 1 cup

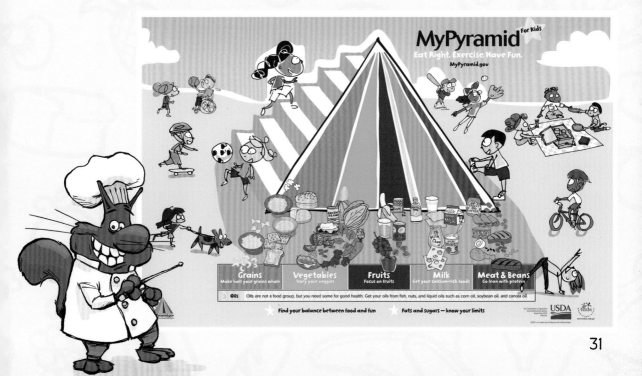

This book provides general dietary information for children ages 5–9 in accordance with the MyPyramid guidelines created by the United States Department of Agriculture (USDA).

Find activities, games, and more at www.brianpcleary.com

The information in this book is not intended as medical advice. Anyone with food allergies or sensitivities should follow the advice of a physician or other medical professional.

ABOUT THE AUTHOR, ILLUSTRATOR & CONSULTANT

BRIAN P. CLEARY is the author of the Words Are Categorical®, Math Is Categorical®, Adventures in Memory™, Sounds Like Reading®, and Food Is CATegorical™ series, as well as several picture books and poetry books. He lives in Cleveland, Ohio.

MARTIN GONEAU is the illustrator of the Food Is CATegorical™ series. He lives in Trois-Rivières, Québec.

JENNIFER K. NELSON is Director of Clinical Dietetics and Associate Professor in Nutrition at Mayo Clinic in Rochester, Minnesota. She is also a Specialty Medical Editor for nutrition and healthy eating content for MayoClinic.com.

Millbrook Press
A division of Lerner Publishing Group, Inc.
241 First Avenue North
Minneapolis, MN 55401 U.S.A.

Website address: www.lernerbooks.com

Library of Congress Cataloging-in-Publication Data

Cleary, Brian P., 1959–
     Green beans, potatoes, and even tomatoes : what is in the vegetable group? / by Brian P. Cleary ; illustrated by
Martin Goneau ; consultant, Jennifer K. Nelson.
        p.   cm. — (Food Is CATegorical)
     ISBN: 978-1-58013-588-7 (lib. bdgs. : alk. paper)
     1. Vegetables—Juvenile literature. 2. Vegetables in human nutrition—Juvenile literature. I. Goneau, Martin.
II. Nelson, Jennifer K. III. Title.
     TX401.C54 2011
     641.3'5—dc22   2009049592

Manufactured in the United States of America
1 – PC – 7/15/10